WEAVING WITH CANE AND REED

This graceful basket was woven by the author. The directions for the circular openwork are included in the book.

WEAVING
WITH
CANE
AND REED

MODERN BASKETRY

GRETE KRONCKE

 VAN NOSTRAND REINHOLD COMPANY
NEW YORK   CINCINNATI   TORONTO   LONDON   MELBOURNE

VAN NOSTRAND REINHOLD COMPANY Regional Offices:
New York   Cincinnati   Chicago   Millbrae   Dallas

VAN NOSTRAND REINHOLD COMPANY International Offices:
London   Toronto   Melbourne

Copyright © 1968 by Litton Educational Publishing, Inc.
Library of Congress Catalog Card Number 67-24695
ISBN 0-442-112440

Printed in Great Britain by Jolly and Barber Ltd, Rugby,
Warwickshire.
Edited in English by Clara Fried Zwiebel

PUBLISHED BY VAN NOSTRAND REINHOLD COMPANY
450 West 33rd Street, New York, N.Y. 10001

Published simultaneously in Canada by
VAN NOSTRAND REINHOLD Ltd.

16 15 14 13 12 11 10 9 8 7 6 5 4 3

Contents

Preface

Basketry is a remarkable craft! Many people are rather skeptical about the material at first, and this, perhaps, is not surprising as it does seem stiff and unresponsive, just dry grass, really! I, myself, felt this way for years until, as a professional occupational therapist, I was actually forced to work with it.

At a recreation center for senior citizens where a variety of craftwork is done, newcomers are greeted by others in the workshop with the words: "Don't start at the basketry table, or you'll never get away!" As soon as you try it yourself you will understand exactly what was meant. There is something about cane and reed that entices you to keep on working with it.

Basket weaving is easy to do, and you can make useful and attractive gifts at a reasonable cost. There are infinite possibilities of variation. You will get an idea of some of these by looking through the designs in this book.

The dyed winding reed and round reed may lure you into an exploratory trip to a Natural History Museum to observe the ethnological collections which will surely inspire you. Museums and books of woven native artifacts are also extremely good as a source of ideas—here you can study how both materials and patterns are coordinated. One can learn a great deal from the way in which the colors are combined in these magnificent, primitive pieces. Warm browns, blues, and greens are the predominant colors used in combination with black and white, but since both primary and pastel colors are now available, any color scheme is currently possible.

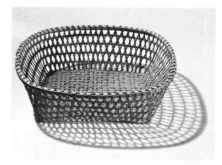

An example of primitive basketry with delicate and gracious openwork weave. It can be seen in the National Museum in Copenhagen, and is the prototype for the reed weaving in this book.

Extremely decorative in design and pattern, this Indian basket from the same museum's ethnographic collection is woven in two colors and has a very delicate border.

Several of the projects in this book are really very easy to make, and for this reason, they are excellent projects for beginners. After trying some of these, you will want to go on to the more difficult pieces. The more you work with these materials, and the more deeply involved with their possibilities you become, the more enjoyment you will find.

Material

Round reed comes from the core of the rattan palm, a tropical climbing plant with thorny shoots that can grow to a length of 500 feet.

The inner pulp of these shoots is composed of long fibers.

The preparation of basketry reed is done by peeling off the bark, thorns, and leaves by pulling these thorny stalks through a notch cut into a nearby tree. This exposes the glossy surface or outer rind. It is then peeled off in long strips and used as cane for weaving chair seats, etc. Special cutting machines slice the center pulp into round and flat reeds of various thicknesses or into winding reed. The heavier winding reed is always flat on one surface and convex on the other (see bottom drawing) and is used for weaving and particularly for wrapping around handles.

Round reed is available in thicknesses from Nos. 00 to 10; winding reed comes in narrow (approx. $\frac{1}{8}''$), and wide (from $\frac{3}{16}''$ to $\frac{1}{4}''$). Some hobby shops carry only one size of winding reed (see drawings).

If you are going to make several baskets it is cheaper to buy round reed by the pound. Winding reed is sold in 300 ft. bundles or hanks and you will profit by buying the best quality. Prepared kits, with all the necessary material included, are also widely available at hobby shops.

Drawings show round reed in various available thicknesses. The lower two pieces are winding reed, which comes in narrow and wide widths, approximately $\frac{1}{8}''$, $\frac{3}{16}''$, and $\frac{1}{4}''$. Shown actual size.

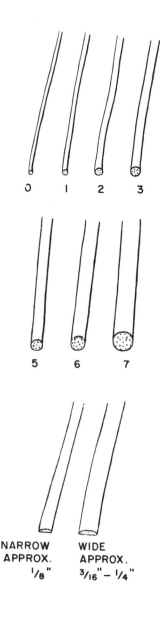

0   1   2   3

5   6   7

NARROW
APPROX.
$\frac{1}{8}''$

WIDE
APPROX.
$\frac{3}{16}'' - \frac{1}{4}''$

9

Working with Reed

Reed is a very supple material, but it is necessary to dampen it well before you work or it will break. Also, it is easier to get an even weave when the reed is wet. The thicker the reed, the longer it should be soaked. The thinner reed (No. 0) need only soak about 2 minutes while heavier reed (No. 2) should be left in the bath at least 5 minute to absorb an adequate amount of moisture before it will be supple enough to work with. As you work it should be redampened as soon as it begins to feel dry.

While you work, therefore, it is very necessary to have a tub of warm water nearby, and it is a good idea to use a sheet of plastic or waxed paper to cover your worktable.

Soak only the amount of reed you will shortly be using as the reed will darken and will also fray easily if it is left too long in the water.

When the basket has been woven and dried, it should be lightly singed with a methylated spirit lamp or Bunsen burner flame to remove the small "fraying whiskers" which will result from handling while weaving. In this process be careful not to discolor the reed by applying too much heat.

If some of the vertical stakes have a tendency to slip out, or if, for some other reason, you want to fasten the reeds, you can use a cellulose or resin glue. The latter is, unfortunately, water-soluble and thus not practical for use in a handbag or market basket. Spread the glue on the back of the place you wish to fasten. Perhaps you will need to spread the reed a little apart in that area, and then reclamp the glued piece with a clothespin (which is a very useful basketry tool) until it has dried.

When the glue has dried and the reed ends have been evenly trimmed, lacquer the basket with a thin solution of cellulose lacquer and thinner (about half of each) both to protect the work, and by means of the resultant gloss, to bring out the surface color nuances.

These liquids are quite flammable and harmful when inhaled, thus it is recommended that you work in a well-ventilated room and, of course, avoid any open flame. Particular caution and adult supervision should be used if children are working with lacquer and thinners.

Dyeing the Winding Reed and Round Reed

Several of the projects in this book are made with combinations of dyed reed. This looks attractive and bright and the different patterns stand out and are more clearly recognized. It is not difficult to dye the reed yourself. Simply use the ordinary fabric dyes that you would use for curtains, etc. which come in so many colors. Wood stains are not recommended for this craft material.

Before dyeing rinse the naturally colored reed in warm water to remove any remnants of chlorine or acid, which were probably used in the manufacture of the reed during the first cleaning. If these chemicals are not removed the cane will not absorb the dye colors as well. Reed is available in its natural beige color and in white reed which has been bleached.

The natural color reed is better suited to dyeing than is the white as certain materials are used in the bleaching process which make it difficult for the dye to penetrate the reed. With the natural colored material the dye colors will also appear warmer.

In dyeing reed at home it is necessary to accomplish this with as little mess as possible. You should be prepared with an enameled basin or something similar, which will be easy to rinse and does not absorb the dye, a large bucket for rinsing, a large tin can or some other disposable container for mixing the dye, and a long stick to remove the finished, dyed material from the dye bath.

Place the basin in the sink, which has previously been well-lined with newspaper to protect the porcelain. Fill the rinsing bucket with cold water and place it on newspapers spread out nearby on the floor.

Dissolve the dye powder in boiling water following package directions. When it is completely dissolved, add it, together with a tablespoon of kitchen salt, to the warm water in the basin in suitable proportions. The warmer the water the better it will dye the material. You can test-dye a small piece of the winding reed to see the color and make certain it is that which you had in mind. The color will usually be somewhat lighter when it dries. The longer you leave the reed in the dye bath, the more color it will absorb. You can mix the dye colors to get the red-brown color which is often used in basketry, by mixing red and brown dye.

When the color bath is ready, lay the previously well-rinsed reed in the basin. It should remain there about 10 minutes; you might turn it over now and then to get an even color. At the same time check to see that the color has not become too dark. The stiffer winding reed which has a tendency to float, can be held securely below the surface in the dye bath, with a heavy object. You can dye about 7 to 8 oz. of reed with one small package of dye.

Using a long stick move the dyed reed carefully over into the rinsing bucket. You can now put another batch of reed in the dye, letting it stay in a bit longer, although it still will probably come out a little lighter than the first batch. This color variation will afford pretty color effects.

The dyed reed should be rinsed in cold water several times. Add a little vinegar to the last batch to "set" the color. Lay the reed out to dry on layers of newspaper or you may hang it up to dry.

It is easiest to dye a large amount or even several colors while you are at it. You will then have a generous supply to work with and a good selection of lengths to choose from. Even small left-overs in various colors can be worked into interesting small baskets or napkin rings.

Wood Bases

Wood bases are practical for some of the baskets. You can either buy the finished bases at a hobby shop or crafts supplier or you can make them yourself. Use ¼″ to ⅜″ plywood. Draw the desired shape directly on the wood and saw it out with a coping saw. Drill the holes for the upright stakes—the correct size and number for your project. The holes are usually ⅝″ or ½″ apart and must be uneven in number for weaving. Sand the wood base smooth with fine sandpaper, always lengthwise, with the grain, and give it a few coats of colorless lacquer.

Materials Required

For most of the projects the amount of round reed is given by weight, but as the weight of the winding reed varies a great deal in relation to its length, this measure is given in feet—in a few cases, however, it does appear as approximate weight. The wide winding reed (approx. 3/16″ to ¼″) runs about .07 oz. per yard and the narrower winding reed runs about half that in weight. If you are trying to judge just how much winding reed will be needed for the amount of dye it is safer to figure by the length required for your project.

Procedure

In basket making you always begin at the bottom—either using a wooden base to start or a woven reed base and then proceed up the sides of the basket, ending and finishing off with the top border.

The materials in basketry are used in two different ways: as vertical "stakes," the measured, upright reeds, over and under which you weave; and as long "weavers" which you will wind in and out between these stakes. If you were to compare this procedure to weaving on a loom, the stakes would correspond to the warp and the weavers to the weft.

Usually the stakes are of ordinary round reed, but in a few designs in this book, the winding reed (flat on one side and rounded on the other) is used as the stakes. We then call them winding reed stakes, so that there will be no confusion. In this case the winding reed is cut to a specified length and used as the basic stakes. The weavers used with these winding reed stakes may be either of round reed or of winding reed, depending upon the design. You can also weave the stakes themselves together, as is done in chair caning or caning weave shown on page 86.

Plain Weaving

Plain basket weaving is done either with one or two long weavers crossing alternately over and under the stakes. In weaving with one weaver, an *uneven* number of stakes is required (see Base A, p. 19). Fig. 1 on page 15 shows 5 rows of weaving with one weaver.

You weave with two weavers only when you have an *equal* number of stakes. Always weave with the innermost or lowest weaver first, and then the upper one (see Base B, p. 21). The drawing in Fig. 2 on page 15 shows 5 double rows of weaving.

To do pairing (see page 17), and vertical pattern weaving (see p. 66), always weave with two weavers of round or winding reed.

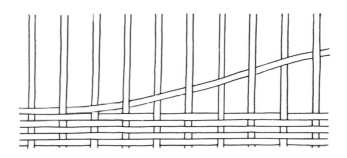

Fig. 1

Weaving with one weaver.

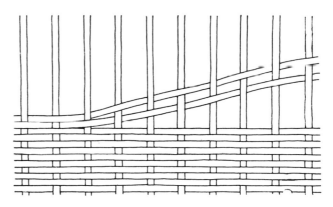

Fig. 2

Weaving with two weavers.

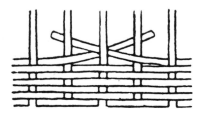

Fig. 3

Joining round reed.

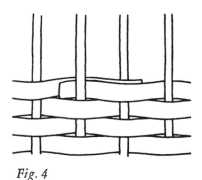

Fig. 4

Joining winding reed.

Helpful Hints

TRIMMING ROUND AND WINDING REEDS should be done so that the ends rest against a stake on the wrong side of the work and are long enough so that they will not slip through to the front.

SMALL PLASTIC CLOTHESPINS are practical for fastening the corners while setting-up the base. Because of their smaller size they are preferable to ordinary wood clothespins, and since these come in bright colors you may use them in a particular color as markers for counting.

WINDING REED FOR HANDLES should be rolled into a coil and fastened with a few clothespins. It is then much easier to handle, curling readily, when you are winding with it.

JOINING THE WINDING REED WHILE WINDING. If it is necessary to join the winding reed while winding a handle, it can be done by letting it lie doubled for about $5/16''$ on the back. Fasten the joint with a clothespin, and later, glue it into place.

JOINING WINDING REED WHILE WEAVING. Double it over 2 stakes to hold it tightly pressed at two points as shown in Fig. 4.

JOINING WITH ROUND REED. When your round reed weaver runs out before the project is finished, pick up a new piece and begin weaving with it, letting the new one cross in front of the old one behind a stake or pair of stakes at the back of the work, leaving the remaining ends resting against a stake (see Fig. 3). When the work is finished you can then trim off the extra ends.

PAIRING. Arrange 2 weavers of round reed in adjacent spaces between two pairs of stakes. Take the weaver farthest to the left and bring it in front of the first pair of stakes, over the second weaver, and behind the second pair of stakes, then out again to the front. Then take the second weaver which is now the farthest behind and bring it in front of the second pair of stakes, back of the next pair and also out to the front. Make sure that the weaver farthest left always crosses over the other weaver. Continue in this manner all the way around (see Fig. 5). Finish by inserting the ends behind the stakes where you started.

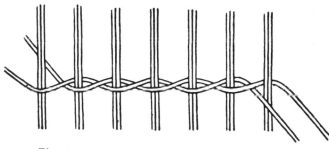

Fig. 5

Pairing

Weaving Wood Based Baskets

It is easiest for a beginner to start from a wood base, and this will be the first project discussed:

1) Sand the base with fine sandpaper, and lacquer it with a mixture of cellulose lacquer and thinner (about half of each). Notice any special warning instructions on the container.

2) Soak the stakes in water for about 5 minutes, and insert them in the holes in the base, leaving about $3\frac{1}{8}''$ projecting from the bottom. The longer ends are the stakes you will be weaving over later.

3) Weaving the base border (Fig. 6). Take one stake and bend it down under the first stake to the left, over the next stake and behind the third. Continue treating each stake in the same manner. The last stakes are inserted in the ones first woven, as if they were still upright.

4) For plain weaving (p. 14) use well-dampened reed which is loosely woven over and under the stakes so that it lies in zigzags around the stakes, which must not be bent. The weaving should be quite loose, as the baskets are either woven straight up or flare slightly outward. They should never be woven so that they curve inward. Weave with the winding reed in the same manner, only continue checking to see that you have the curved side on the correct side of the basket. The changeover from round reed to winding reed can be made in the same way as in joining weavers—by crossing them behind a stake (Fig. 3; p. 16). See joining of winding reed, Fig. 4; p. 16.

Several different borders for finishing the basket are described on pages 23 to 27. When the basket is completed the ends of the round or winding reed are trimmed so that they rest properly against a stake, otherwise they may slip through to the front. For added safety in construction it is important to glue these ends to the stakes with a little dab of resin glue, and let it dry well before lacquering.

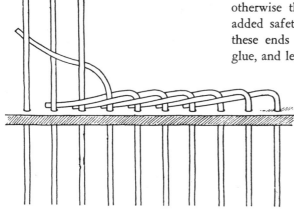

Fig. 6

Weaving a base border on a wood base with pre-bored holes.

Woven Bases

When you have gained some experience in working with plain wood bases, you should be ready to
tackle the more demanding, but far prettier woven
bases. Several different examples of woven bases
are explained on the following pages. The first bases
are woven with one weaver (Bases A) and the other
set of bases are woven with two weavers (Bases B).

Setting-up Bases A

On a table or any flat surface lay out the total
number of stakes required. It is easiest to start weaving the base by arranging or "setting-up" all the
stakes that go in one direction. Then, at a right
angle, weave-in two pairs of stakes which will secure
the previous stakes. Continue weaving-in one pair
of stakes at a time, alternating the crossings of the
preceding pair until all are woven. Clamp the corners
with small plastic clothespins. Adjust the stakes so
that opposite ends protruding from the base are of
equal length. Using a long weaver, work well down
into the corners and let it curve out along the sides.
This long weaver forms the circular base. Check for
roundness by placing a round object, such as a saucer,
over the base. When one row has been completed,
insert an *extra pair* of stakes at one corner. In this
way you will have the uneven total number of stakes
necessary to enable you to continue weaving with
one weaver.

Base A 1:

Set-up the base with four pairs of stakes in one
direction and weave-in four pairs in the other direction. Place the stakes fairly close together, and weave
once around with a weaver. Then insert an extra
pair of stakes as shown in the drawing on the right,
A 1. As you weave each new row it should alternate
with the preceding one over and under the stakes.

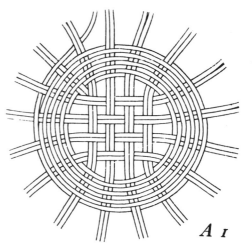

A 1

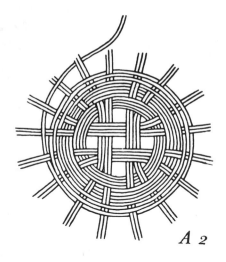

A 2

BASE A 2:

Set-up a base of 2 groups of 4 stakes in each direction. Place the groups of stakes close together. With one long weaver work four rows over and under each of the four stakes each time, keeping the woven rows as close together as possible. In basketry this is called *randing* and the woven section is called the *rand*. Soak the weaver extremely well and bend it carefully all the way around the last pair of stakes, now weaving in the opposite direction for four more rows. The stakes which were previously outside will now be on the inside of your work. See drawing A 2. Next, bend the weaver you are using back around the stakes randing in the same direction as you did when you began, after inserting an extra pair of stakes. At the same time divide the other groups of stakes into pairs, so that you have 17 pairs in all, as shown in the drawing. Continue randing, following the directions for your project.

BASE A 3:

Weave this base in the same manner as in A 2, adding 4 more stakes in each direction.

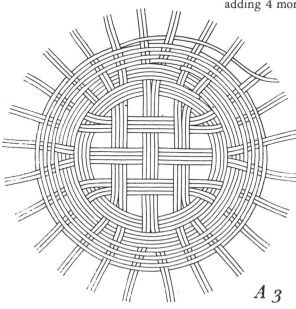

A 3

Setting-up Bases B

The following group of B-bases are woven to correspond to those in group A, except that instead of inserting an extra stake to provide an uneven number of stakes, here you will rand with two weavers. They are woven in alternate openings. This is clearly shown in drawing B 2, where one weaver is colored black.

BASE B 1:

Set-up the stakes as for Base A 1, but immediately start the randing with two long weavers.

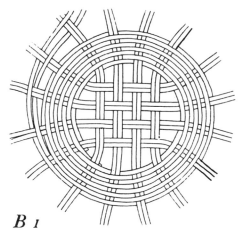

B 1

BASE B 2:

Set-up the stakes and weave the first two groups of 4 rows exactly as for Base A 2. The second weaver, shown in black on drawing B 2, is then inserted.

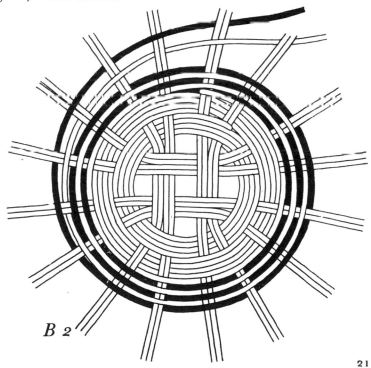

B 2

Base B 3:

The base is started exactly as in Base A 3; the second weaver is later inserted as described in B 2.

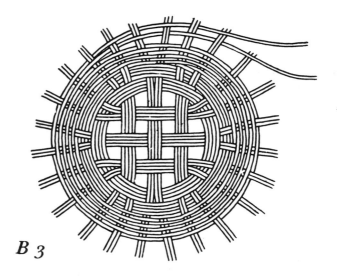

B 3

Basket Borders

There are many decorative possibilities in making the borders as well as the bases, using this material. The borders also serve the practical purpose of finishing off the basket while, at the same time, locking the weave.

Scalloped Borders

BORDER 1 A:

This is the simplest kind of border. Using a knitting needle to force the space open, insert one upright stake down into the weave along the side of its neighboring stake. Make sure that all the ends have been trimmed to the same length.

BORDER 1 B:

This is made with double stakes (pairs) which are inserted in the same manner as was Border 1 A. (See basket, p. 36.)

Additional variations of the scalloped border are shown on pages 44 and 48.

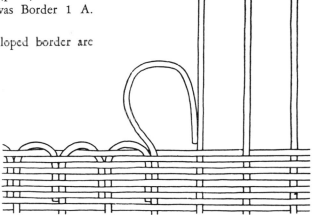

Scalloped Border 1 A.

Braided Borders

This is a very firm border and is well-suited to finishing a basket where the edge must have extra firmness. You can form this border so that it is at a right angle to the side of the basket forming a lip (see coffee baskets p. 65), or you can keep the stakes held down somewhat during the weaving to make the edge slant inward (Wastepaper basket, p. 61). The right-angle border is also useful for supporting a lid that will rest on it. You can vary the width of this border by weaving over and under more or fewer pairs of stakes in the second row, as seen with three pair in Border 2 A, and four in Border 2 B.

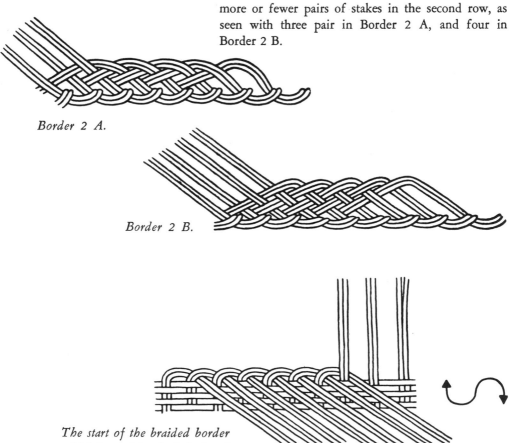

Border 2 A.

Border 2 B.

The start of the braided border which is used for both 2 A and 2 B.

The beginning of the two following borders are alike:

When the basket itself has been woven, re-wet the border edge completely. Now, weave the first row of the border: Using a pair of stakes, place these to the right and behind the next pair of stakes, then bring them out toward the front. Take this second pair of stakes, and in the same manner, place it, in turn, behind the third pair and then also out toward the front. Continue in this way all around the basket working to the right. The last pair of stakes is inserted into the loop made by the first pair with which you began the border.

Now work the second row. Turn the work so that the opening of the basket is facing you.

SECOND STAGE OF BORDER 2 A:

Weave the first pair of stakes behind the second pair to the left, over the third pair and leave them pointed downward on the outside of the basket, below the border. (2A) Weave the second pair of stakes under the third pair, over the fourth pair, and under the fifth pair, then down, just as you placed the first pair. Continue in this manner weaving to the left, all the way around. Finish by slipping the last pair of stakes through the first pair of woven stakes in the same fashion as was done for the rest.

SECOND STAGE OF BORDER 2 B:

Weave the first pair of stakes over the second pair, under the third pair, over the fourth pair and then straight down along the outside of the basket below the edge. The second pair is woven over the third pair, under the fourth, over the fifth, and again down into the outside of the basket. If you wish the border to be still wider, simply increase the number of paired stakes over and under which you weave with each pair of stakes.

Madeira Border

BORDER 3:

The Madeira border is woven with flat winding reed, as indicated in the drawing. Since they are flat the reeds must be creased at the top to lie smoothly. Finish by neatly weaving the last winding reed down into the first one woven as if they were still upright.

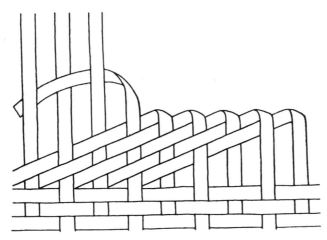

Madeira, Border 3.

Inverted Border

BORDER 4:

The inverted border is used, among others, on baskets with diagonal weaving (pp. 57 and 61). When the weaving is completed, the ends of the winding reed, which is used in this instance, should be well-dampened, carefully bent, and turned down on the inside surface of the basket directly on top of the winding reed stakes. Use a knitting needle to guide and help you to insert these ends through the weaving. They should go under at least two rows. As shown in the drawing, each stroke of this inverted border will be at a different level because it follows the pattern of the weaving. This same principle can be used for a border on any piece of plain weaving which is evenly worked over and under, using either round or winding reed. The inverted border works out quite evenly and should end deeply down through the whole woven piece for extra support. It is invariably worked on the inside of the basket.

Inverted Border 4.

Projects

After having read the preceding section, you are ready to begin making the projects. The first pieces have wood bases, which are best, as we have already suggested, for beginner's use as they are easy to work with and produce quick results.

Wastepaper Basket

(wood base)

in three colors

Height—12"

Diameter at top—12"

This attractive wastepaper basket can be color-keyed to any room decor. It is very stable and not difficult to make. This one was woven using natural colored round reed with stripes of black and rust-brown winding reed. It would be just as handsome in natural round reed with black and white winding reed or any other combination. The basket's unusual shape is the result of starting the weave on a square wooden base then continuing the weave upward, rounding and expanding the circumference as the work progresses.

Materials: A ½" thick wood base, about 6¾" square with 33 pre-bored holes for the stakes (8,8,8,9). You will need approx. 1¾ oz. of natural color round reed No. 3; and approx. 4½" oz. of round reed No. 2 as well as 85 feet of rust-brown, plus 40 feet of wide, black winding reed. Cut 33 stakes about 17¾" in length, of the No. 3 reed.

Follow the weaving directions on pages 17-18.

Weave 6 rows with round reed, 5 rows with rust-brown winding reed; again do 6 rows of round reed, 3 rows of black winding reed, then 6 rows of round reed to complete the pattern.

Continue this pattern until there are 4 bands of the black winding reed and 5 bands of the rust-brown reed. Finish off the top portion with 14 rows of natural round reed. Border 1 A on page 23 provides a sturdy and long-lasting reinforcement besides being an attractive edging.

It is important to keep a constant check on the shape of the basket, always maintaining an equal distance between the stakes all the way around. This spacing is narrow at the base, about ¾", and it will increase evenly between each upright stake to a width of about 1¼" at the top.

Small Handy Basket *(wood base)*

Height without handle—4½"

With handle—11"

This handy little basket has many uses in the home or in the garden. The same design procedure used here may also be used in making much larger baskets, both round and oval. If you do not like a bright colored winding reed, you can achieve very handsome results by combining white winding reed with natural round reed.

Materials: A ½" thick wood base about 6¾" in diameter with 23 pre-bored holes; 23 stakes, each 10" long are cut from No. 2 round reed; approx. 66 feet of natural round reed, No. 1; 12 feet of white; and 24 feet of narrow blue winding reed.

Handle: 2 lengths of round reed No. 6, cut 22" long; 12 feet of white winding reed; and about 11" of blue.

Follow the general weaving directions given on pages 17-18.

Weave straight for 8 rows with round reed,* 1 row—white winding reed; 4 rows—blue winding reed; 1 row—white winding reed; and 6 rows—natural round reed.* Repeat pattern between ** until 3 colored bands are formed then finish the top with 10 rows of natural round reed using Border 1 A on page 23.

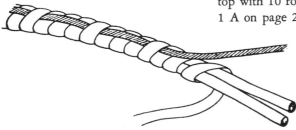

Handle for Small Basket: Here the blue winding reed goes over 3 and under 1 as the handle is wound. But you can also wind it so that the winding reed color alternates over 1 and under 1 or 2.

Handle: Insert the two thick, round reed pieces about 2⅜" down into the weaving at either side of the basket. (Measure to find the center if there is an uneven count of border loops.) Wind the handle with white winding reed and lace it decoratively with the 11" length of blue (see drawing).

Insert any remaining ends down into the sides of the basket and glue them into place.

Market Basket *(wood base)*

Height without handle—10¼"

With handle—17¾"

This market basket is not difficult to weave, although it looks very professional. It is an excellent project for a beginner provided the directions are carefully followed.

Materials: An oval wooden base, approx. 5″ x 10½″ with 41 evenly distributed, pre-bored holes (15,15,6,5). 41 Stakes of No. 3 round reed, each approx. 15¾″ long (approx. 1.75 oz.). For the weaving you will need about 66 feet of natural round reed No. 2 (approx. 2 oz.); and about 132 feet of wide, natural winding reed (approx. 3 oz.).

Use No. 7 round reed for the handle: 1 piece 35½″ long and 2 pieces 25½″ long, also about 16½ feet of wide winding reed with 2 pieces of No. 2 round reed about 21½″ in length.

Follow the directions on pages 17-18.

Weave 8 rows quite loosely using the round reed, and then 43 rows with flat winding reed, curving the basket outward a little at the top (see photograph). At the top edge finish with 14 rows of round reed, and insert the stakes well down into the winding reed and trim them as in Border 1 A on page 23.

The handle is probably the most awkward part to make, but if you find this method too difficult, you can substitute the previous handle on page 30. The longest handle piece is inserted about 7⅛″ down through the weaving at the center of each of the widest sides; the two shorter pieces are inserted on either side of this first piece, about 2½″ down into the weave. The two No. 2 round reed pieces are then laid over the first three which are held closely together. Weave the long winding reed around the handle over the three basic pieces while alternating over and under the two shorter loose pieces (see drawing). Insert any ends down into the basket weave. Glue the handle in place with Elmer's glue, reaching neatly through the weave.

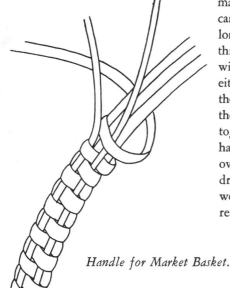

Handle for Market Basket.

Bread Basket *(wood base)*

Height (approx.)—3"

Base—5" x 8"

Top—8" x 11"

This well-designed bread basket is very useful with its outward sloping sides and spacious capacity, yet at the same time, it is not at all difficult to make, and therefore is an excellent project for beginners. You must try to keep the proper outwardly-slanting shape, however, as your work progresses.

Materials: A wooden base 5″ x 8″ with 37 evenly spaced, pre-bored holes (12,12,7,6); approx. 1.75 oz. of natural round reed No. 2; about 33 feet of narrow white winding reed, plus two pieces of round reed No. 6 about 7″ long for 2 handles.

Cut 37 stakes, of natural round reed No. 3 to a length of 11″.

Carefully follow the directions on pages 17-18.

After making the border all around the base, weave 8 rows of round reed, 5 rows of winding reed, 5 rows of round reed, 5 rows of winding reed, and lastly, 8 rows of round reed. Finish with Border 2 B, which should be turned outward. Weave every successive row loosely so the basket's sides will flare outward.

Insert the two round reed handles into the ends of the basket after wrapping them with white winding reed, and glue them into place.

Wine Bottle Jacket

Height—4″

Wine bottles at the dinner table are apt to stain the cloth. You can avoid this by weaving one of these smart jackets for them which will not obscure the label which you may want to show. They are usually made of natural colored reed but you may prefer a combination of color and white winding reed. Napkin rings, to match and further complement the table decor, are described on page 41. These baskets might be grouped, 2 or 3 together, to hold ketchup, mustard etc. and provided with one long handle in the center, with a loop on top.

Materials: 66 feet of white round reed No. 1 (approx. 9 oz.); 9 feet of blue; and 6 feet of narrow red winding reed. Cut 16 stakes 13¾″ in length.

Set-up the base in pairs of stakes (A 1, p. 19). Weave one row and insert another pair of stakes, then continue in plain weave with one weaver until the base is the correct size to fit your bottle. Turn the stakes upward, and weave 8 rows of round reed, 3 rows of blue winding reed, 5 rows of round reed; 3 rows of red winding reed, and lastly, 5 rows of round reed. Continue in this pattern until there are 3 blue and 2 red bands. Finish the top with 8 rows of round reed and Border 1 B. Insert the stakes well down into the weaving to the topmost blue band, then cut them off on the inside.

It is not necessary to cut off the reed each time a few rows of winding reed are woven in, you can simply leave the round reed on the inside of the weaving and pick it up again when you are ready to use it.

To give the basket a more stable standing surface, dampen the finished basket and press the base slightly inward so it is convex when it dries.

Two-tone Trivet

Diameter—7″

Two colors make this gay and vivid trivet or hot pad. It is easy to do and in addition the pattern will serve for making other flat, woven rounds which can be adapted for use as coasters, flowerpot stands, etc. See photograph on page 33.

Materials: About 43 feet of white round reed and 17 feet of blue round reed, both No. 2.

Cut 16 stakes each 14″ long and set-up the base as shown in B 2, on page 21. Begin with plain weaving alternating the white and blue weavers. This results in a strong pattern which resembles radiating beams. To finish, insert each successive stake down alongside its neighboring stake completely through the woven piece toward the center and cut them off closely at the back.

Large, Handled Basket

Height without handle—10″

With handle—18½″

This is a very useful basket for many things—for marketing, knitting, mending or as a catch-all. It is so easy to carry around and so spacious that you will soon find it is indispensable.

Materials: About 94 yards of round reed No. 2, 100 feet of wide winding reed and 2 pieces of No. 7 round reed, 30″ long, for the handle. Cut 24 stakes 40″ long and 2 stakes 19½″ long. Make Base A 3 arranging the stakes as closely together as possible. Weave until the flat base measures 7″ in diameter.

Wet the base thoroughly and place it upside-down on the worktable so that the stakes can now be carefully turned up around a nail or an ice pick close to the edge of the first row of weaving and at right angles to the base. Gather loosely and tie the long ends of the stakes together to dry. When the piece is dry, dip and re-dampen all the long stakes, taking care not to wet the base, then untie the bundle. Weave 6 rows upward, in plain weaving.

Now insert a knitting needle or a similar tool along one pair of stakes in the vertically turned foot-piece edge, and taking hold of the nearest stake of the pair of stakes next to the tool, insert the stake into the place opened by the knitting needle. Now take the second stake of that pair and insert it between stake number 1 and the upright pair (Fig. 1). Continue in this manner until all the stakes have been turned in and inserted. The loops created in this manner form the foot-piece of the basket.

Turn the work over again and weave the basket itself using the long reed weaver which remains sticking up from the back where you left it earlier. Be sure to pick up your weaving correctly, in the right space, so that it continues from where you stopped earlier in the proper order. It is important to press the first row of weaving extra tightly down into the previously woven portion behind the upright stakes (Fig. 2).

Now continue weaving loosely so that the sides of the basket will bulge slightly outward. Weave until you have 17 double rows, including the foot edge. Then weave 15 double rows with the winding reed always remembering to keep the rounded side of this outward, and to keep the weaving loose so that the basket continues to flare outward.

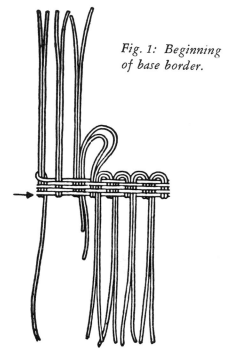

Fig. 1: Beginning of base border.

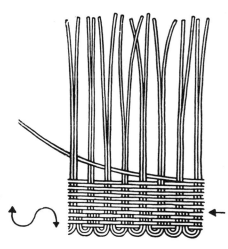

Fig. 2: Turn work and continue weaving.

The height of the basket should be about 7½" at this point, and the interior circumference at the top of this weaving should be about 32½".

Next, weave 13 double rows of round reed, and, as shown in the illustration, make this part slant sharply outward. Finish with Border 1 B, and insert the stakes well down into the section woven with the winding reed and lastly, clip them off inside.

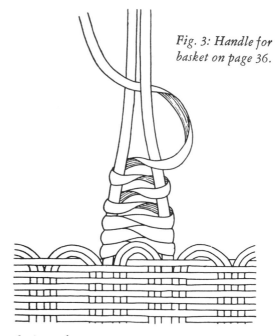

Fig. 3: Handle for basket on page 36.

Handle: Insert the 2 No. 7 round reed pieces about 2" down into the topmost portion of the weaving with one border loop in-between each piece of the handle. If there is an uneven number of loops, you must measure to find the best-balanced position for the handles. Weave 9 rows around these with winding reed bringing the two handle pieces closer and closer together, while keeping the rounded edges of the winding reed turned outward (see drawing). At the center wind around the two handle pieces together. Approaching the other side, repeat the procedure in reverse. Glue the handles in place.

Small Articles for the Breakfast Table

Here are some useful items for the breakfast table. The napkin rings can be made with stripes of different colors for each family member, with egg cups to match. The little "vitamin basket" is intended to hold the perennial vitamin pill bottles—to be whisked away after the meal.

These pieces may be made of remnants.

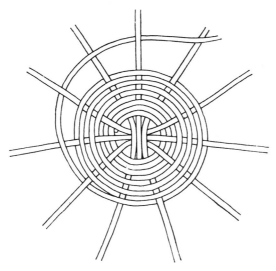

*Base for
egg cup.*

EGG CUP. Cut 6 stakes 15¾" long of No. 1 round reed. Lay three stakes on the table and place three other stakes over these at a right angle. Weave 3 rows around, over, and under the groups of three stakes (see drawing). Snip off one stake so that the weaving can be continued on 5, going over and under one stake at a time (plain weaving) until the bottom measures about 1½". Turn the stakes upward, and weave 8 more rows with round reed, 3 rows with winding reed, and 6 rows again with round reed. Insert the stakes alongside their neighboring stakes completely down and projecting past the bottom of the egg cup so that these ends may be used to weave a foot as was done under the wooden base in Fig. 6 on page 18.

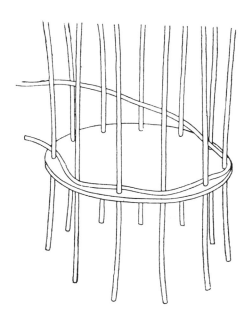

Start weaving the napkin ring using a cardboard disc as a pattern form.

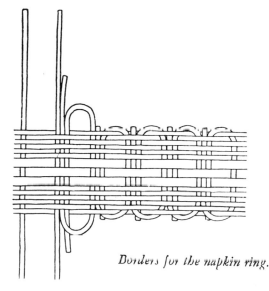

Borders for the napkin ring.

NAPKIN RING. This is woven using a small, hard, $3\frac{1}{8}''$ cardboard disc as a control form. Draw a circle with a $1\frac{1}{2}''$ radius, cut out the disc and punch 11 evenly spaced holes around the edge (see drawing). Clip 11 stakes, $4\frac{3}{4}''$ in length, from No. 1 round reed and insert them $\frac{1}{3}$ their length in each hole. Weave 6 rows with No. 1 round reed and 3 rows with colored narrow winding reed then 6 more rows, again with round reed. Pull the work away from the paper disc and insert each of the stakes beside its neighboring stake on both sides to complete the napkin ring, as shown in the drawing, then clip off the uneven ends.

Using wide white winding reed cut 9 stakes 16″ long and 18 stakes 12″ long. Set-up the base so that it will be about 2¾″ x 5½″. Follow the directions on page 53. After the pairing, weave 2 rows in diagonal weaving with white winding reed and 6 rows with green, then 2 rows again, with white. The diagonal weaving here is done by crossing over 3 and under 1 stake, but otherwise it is woven in the same manner as ordinary diagonal weaving. End with Border 4.

Fashion the handle from 2 pieces of white winding reed about 11″ in length which are placed with flat sides together. These should be glued together. Insert the handle in the weave at the center of the long sides of the basket and glue into place. Give the handle an extra coat of lacquer when lacquering the basket.

Oblong Basket

Height without handle—1¾″

With handle—8″

Size at top—about 8¾″ x 15½″

Baskets with Curved, Forked Handles

These baskets have a modern, architectural look and interestingly, they both compliment and soften a modern decor. These are useful for many things; the small one for serving rolls, fruit, or cookies; and the larger one holds sandwiches or is fine for serving cheese.

Materials: Natural colored round reed: about 2 oz. of No. 5, 3 oz. of No. 2, and 4 pieces of No. 6 round reed 23″ long plus 2 long pieces of wide winding reed.

Cut 5 stakes 43″ long and 7 stakes 37½″ long, plus 8 pieces 18″ long to be inserted later; all of No. 5 round reed.

Set-up the base as shown in Fig. 1, p. 45 with the 5 long stakes close together and the 7 stakes woven through them at right angles leaving about 1″ of space in-between. Weave 2 rows around with one weaver, and then continue the weave with 2 weavers, 9 double rows in all, of plain weaving.

Insert the 8 shorter stakes into the rounded ends placing them between the four stakes at each end. Continue weaving over one, under the next, until the base measures approx. 8¾″ x 15½″. Bend the dampened stakes sharply upward and weave 6 double rows. Insert the stakes down through the sides of the basket as shown in Fig. 2, this page. Finish the foot of the basket with the neat edge shown in Fig. 3, this page.

Fig. 2: Inverting stakes to make the top border.

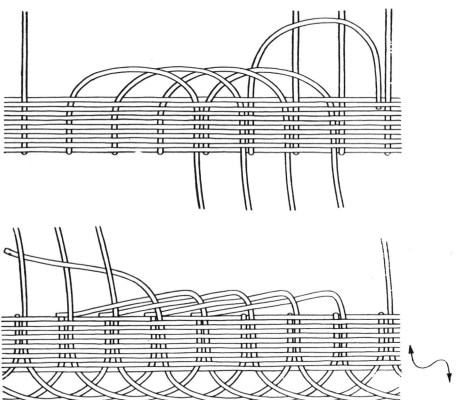

Fig. 3: After inverting the stakes, turn basket over and weave the base border: under one, over one, and back, etc.

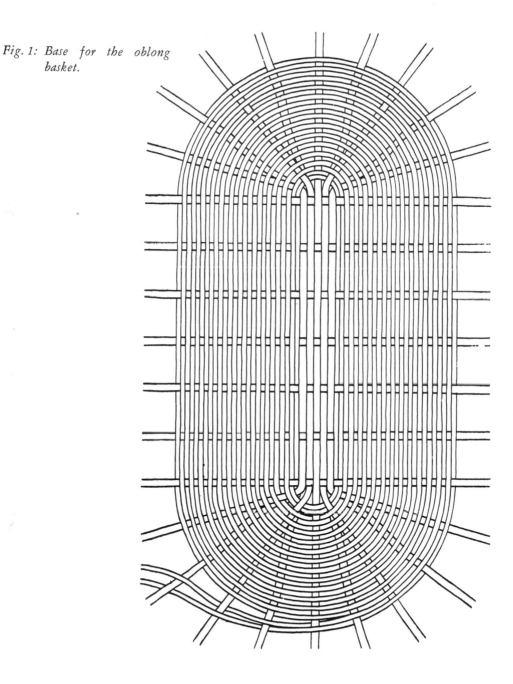

Fig. 1: Base for the oblong basket.

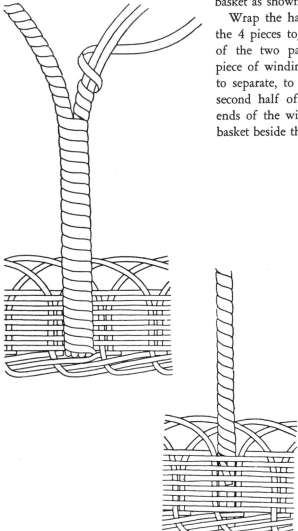

At one end, insert the 4 pieces of round reed approx. 2¾″ down into and beneath the woven base and then turn the handle sharply upward (see drawing) and near the top separate it into two pairs. The two pairs are then inserted in both sides of the basket as shown in the photograph on page 43.

Wrap the handle with winding reed. Go around the 4 pieces together 23 times, and then wind each of the two pairs remembering to insert an extra piece of winding reed in time, about 1″ before it is to separate, to anchor it securely when covering the second half of the divided handle. Insert the last ends of the winding reed down through the woven basket beside the handle. Glue the handle into place.

The opposite end of the handle with winding completed, has been inserted down into the side weave of the basket, as are any ends of the winding reed used to wrap the handle.

46

Materials: 2½ oz. of round reed No. 2; 4 pieces of No. 16 round reed 20″ long, and 2 long, wide, winding reed pieces.

Cut 16 stakes 27½″ long. Set-up base B 2 as on page 21, and weave until the base measures 7⅛″ in diameter. Divide the stakes one by one pairing them and turn the stakes upward. Then weave 10 double rows. Make the rest of the basket in the same way as the Oblong Basket above. (The handle, however, is inserted here only 1½″-2″ into the base.)

Round Bread Basket

Height without handle—2″

With Handle—about 6¾″

Diameter—7½″

Baskets and Hotplate with Circular Openwork

Height: round basket—1"; oval basket—1½"

Diameter: round basket—8¾"; oval basket—11⅜" x 12¼"

Diameter: Hotplate—8"

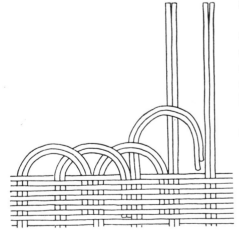

Fig. 1: Border for basket.

Circular Openwork

These are a few new designs using the beautiful circular openwork of basketry and showing several ways in which it is used. Specific directions for this weave are given on page 50.

Materials: Round basket with handle—1½ oz. round reed No. 1; Oval basket—3 oz. of No. 2 round reed; Hotplate Mat—1½ oz. of No. 2 round reed.

The directions given here are for the round basket. The oval basket is woven in the same way, with changes indicated in parenthesis(). Cut 24 stakes 27½" long of No. 1 round reed and set-up base B 3 as on page 22. (28 stakes 31½" long of No. 2 round reed, Fig. 2). Weave until the base measures 6" (6⅜" x 8¾"). Make a row of circular openwork and bend it slightly upward pulling it together with a row of pairing, using the two weavers that were used in weaving the base. The two weavers should now be brought up as inconspicuously as possible behind the circular openwork. Continue weaving for 14 (12) rows allowing the sides of the basket to flare outward a little. Finish the border as shown in Fig. 1 on this page.

The handle for the round basket is made of 2 pieces of No. 6 round reed, 21½" long; the ends are forced through the top woven section of the basket, directly opposite each other. Wind the handle with a long piece of wide winding reed then glue it into place.

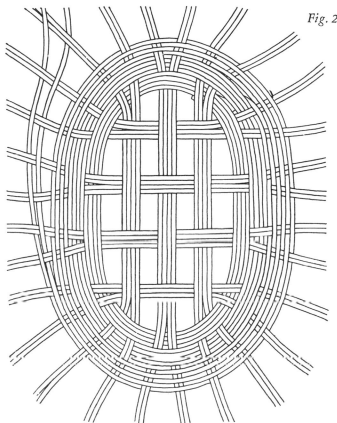

Fig. 2: Base for the oval basket.

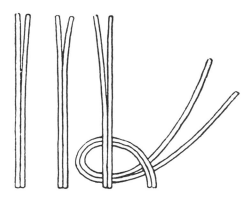

Fig. 3: Beginning of circular openwork.

Hotplate:. This is made exactly in the same way as the basket; it is not flared, however, but simply kept flat. Cut 16 stakes of No. 1 round reed, 26" long. Set-up base B 2 and weave 6 double rows, one row of circular openwork, and a row of pairing; which divides the stakes one by one; and finally, three double rows.

Finish with Border 2A, which should be turned upward to create the raised edge.

MAKING CIRCULAR OPENWORK

The stakes must be kept well-dampened. Start the work by turning one pair of stakes around to the left to form a loop, and bringing the end of the loop back to lie behind the beginning. Hold this loop with your right hand while * the next pair of stakes to the left are in front of the first loop (Fig. 3). With your left hand take this new pair of stakes and make another loop clock-wise, inserting the ends of this loop in from the back through the first loop, over the beginning of the 2nd loop, and again behind the top of the first loop (Fig. 4). Be very careful in pulling these loops to keep the stakes under the circular openwork equidistant in position from each other and not crossing. * Repeat this procedure between ** all the way around the basket. The joint can be completely hidden by taking the two ends left loose from the first pair of stakes and inserting them in the last loop, which is placed behind the first loop, and then down again in the same manner as all the others.

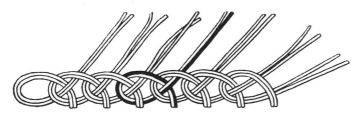

Fig. 4: The circular openwork pattern progression.

Diagonal Brick Pattern Basket

(Wood base)

Height—8¼″

Interlacing the brick pattern for this small basket is fun, and with a little experience a basket made this way will have a uniformly even, but light character. The pattern is open and airy, useful for flowerpot holders, for example, which are also woven on wood bases as is this one.

If you prefer you can omit the lower rows of plain basketweaving and begin with the brick design immediately after weaving the base border, and then a few rows of plain weaving at the top can be done before starting to do the border.

Materials: Use an oval wooden base for the wastepaper basket, approx. 6½" x 10" with 35 pre-bored holes. Cut 35 stakes 20" long of No. 3, or preferably, No. 5 round reed—you will need about 60 feet. For the weavers, about 50 feet of round reed No. 2; and about 83 feet of wide winding reed.

Wet the lower 4" of the stakes thoroughly and insert them in the holes in the base. If it is too difficult to get them through the holes, insert the dry ends first and pull these through, so that the wet part protrudes about 3⅛" under the base. These are then used to weave the base border. Now weave 9 rounds of plain weaving with one weaver to start the basket. Up to this point follow the directions on pages 17-18.

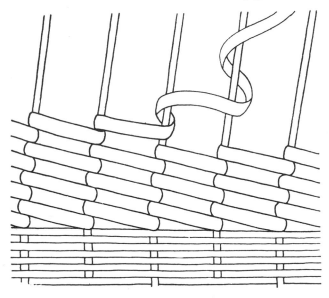

Brick pattern.

BRICK PATTERN: Lay the winding reed behind one stake, over the stake to the right and around it, then over the next and around that (see drawing), keeping the rounded side of the reed to the outside. Continue in this manner all the way around and on all succeeding rows. It takes a little practice to achieve evenness in this pattern. The winding reed must be quite damp and the stakes dry and rigid. You must hold the previous row in place with your left hand when beginning the following one, so that it does not loosen. The stakes will tend to bend a little to the right and you must take care that this trend does not become too pronounced. Weave 18 rows in the brick pattern and finish the top with 14 rows of plain weaving in round reed and end with Border 2B, on page 25.

Weaving a Diagonal Pattern

Cut the required number of stakes and set-up the base (see drawing). The rounded side of the winding reed should be turned up (facing you) while setting-up the base. It is simpler to initially weave 2 winding reeds in each direction over and under each other as indicated by the numbers 1,2,3,4 on the drawing. Be sure to weave the stakes so that you have the same number on each side. The distance between each stake should be approximately the same width as the winding reed used.

When the bottom has been done with two No. 1 round reeds weave in a pairing stroke all the way around (see drawing) to reinforce and firm the base. Then bend the wet stakes sharply up with the rounded side turned outward. You are now ready to weave steadily with a long winding reed in diagonal weaving all the way up the basket sides—over 2, under 2, over 2 (see drawing). Before you have completed one full round weave one of the winding reed stakes back down through the base piece. This is done so that there will be an uneven number of stakes remaining for the weaving. After the weaving has progressed for a few rows, trim off the extra stake so that it is not visible. At the beginning you may find it a little difficult to do the diagonal weaving, as the last woven row has a tendency to loosen and to slip upward, but if you keep your work well-dampened, this problem will be overcome after a few rows. As can be seen in the lower drawing, the weaving advances one stake in each row as it progresses and creates the diagonal pattern. Instructions for joining winding reed are found on page 16.

Remember to keep the stakes completely perpendicular.

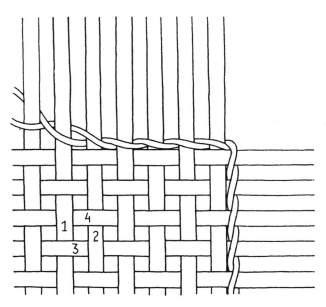

Setting-up the base with winding reed—note numbers.

Diagonal weaving is always done with an uneven number of winding reed stakes—over 2, under 2. This makes the pattern move forward diagonally.

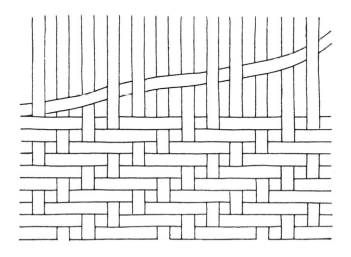

Tote Bag with Diagonal Weave

Height—9"; with handle—18"

The diagonal weave in this basket is clearly seen since natural colored winding reed stakes are used in combination with white winding reed for the weaving. This contrast emphasizes an appearance of depth in the weaving.

Materials: About 116 feet of natural color, wide winding reed and 139 feet of wide, white winding reed.

Cut 10 stakes each 36" long, and 25 stakes 32" in length, all of wide, natural color winding reed. Set-up the base with 10 long pieces in one direction and the 25 shorter ones in the opposite direction. The base should measure about 8¾" x 3½". Check to see that all the stakes are pulled evenly. See the directions on page 53.

Weave a pairing row all the way around using two weavers of No. 1 round reed, then bend the stakes upward, round side facing outward. Weave upward in diagonal weave for 8" curving the weave a little outward for approximately 42 rows.

Finish the top edge with Border 3.

Handle: Use 2 pieces of No. 7 round reed about 30" long. Insert these 4" down into the weaving on either side of the basket. Wind the handle with white winding reed over the natural color reed (see p. 30). Insert the ends and glue the handle firmly into place. When the glue has dried and the basket has been lightly singed, it should be lacquered to keep it clean as well as to refine its smooth feeling and protect your clothes from snagging.

An attractive lining should be provided for the tote bag to prevent small items from dropping through the weave and to minimize the ends of the border weave from snagging things. The lining of

one or two sections can easily be sewn in after seams
and hems are made, to fit snugly at the top and then
gathered slightly along the bottom to fit smoothly.
The center bottom piece is cut to fit the base of the
bag with ¾" seam allowance added. Hand-stitch
the lining to the bag at top, and catch stitch it to
the body at the corners or where necessary to hold it
in place.

Large Flared Basket

Height—4"

Measure at top—12" x 16"

The basket in the picture is woven with black winding reed and has bands of white and rust-brown winding reed. It is also useful as a handiwork basket.

Materials: About 160 feet of black, 26 feet of white, and 28 feet of brown, wide winding reed. Also about 10 feet of black round reed, No. 1 or No. 2.

Using black winding reed cut 23 stakes 30" in length, and 31 stakes 25½" in length. Arrange these with the long stakes all laid in one direction, so that the base will measure about 7½" x 12". Follow the directions on page 53. After a row of pairing, turn the stakes upward, but this time contrary to what has been done before, the flat side of the reed is turned outward since in this basket, with its widely flaring edges, the inner side will be the most visible. The entire basket is done in diagonal weaving and with the rounded side of the reed turned to show in the interior of the basket. Weaving quite loosely so that you will achieve a good flare in the shape, work in the following order: 4 rows — black, 3 rows — white, 3 rows — brown, 1 row — black, 3 rows — white, 3 rows — brown, 1 row — black.

Finish with Border 3, woven so that the stake ends are turned to the outside of the basket.

Lacquer this basket several times so that it becomes quite rigid; the heavy lacquer finish will also make the colors stand out very clearly. Stripes of decorative velvet or silk ribbon may be threaded through the weave and the ends tacked down before inserting the lining.

Utility Basket

Height—9"

Diameter at top—10⅝"

This basket is quite roomy and can be used for many different purposes—to hold the family mending or to hold material for any kind of unfinished handiwork. It is also practical to line it, to protect the contents from snagging on the inside.

Materials: About 200 feet of natural or white, wide winding reed.

For the pattern: 76 feet of brown and 20 feet of red wide winding reeds. Cut 42 winding reed stakes 36″ long.

Set-up the base with 21 stakes in each direction. The square base measures 8″ on each side. Follow the directions on page 53. After a row of pairing, turn the stakes up so that their rounded side is turned outward. Work in diagonal weaving as shown in the illustration. Begin with 9 rows of brown, 3 rows of natural, then a herringbone in red (See p. 63) and continue in this diagonal weave: 3 rows — natural, 5 rows — brown, 3 rows — natural. Work another red herringbone and finish with diagonal weaving, 3 rows of natural and 9 rows of brown which are gradually woven more and more tightly so that the basket curves inward a little at the top. Finish with Border 3, woven straight up. Stake ends should be inserted on the inside of the basket.

Letter Basket

Interior—9″ x 12½″ x 3¼″

This is a low desk basket suitable for holding mail. It can be done in one color or, for example, as it is woven here, in natural colored winding reed with 1 black and 2 brown stripes.

Materials: About 182 feet of natural wide winding reed. For the stripes: Approx. 25 feet of brown and 12½ feet of black wide winding reed. For pairing, about 10 feet of No. 1 round reed.

Cut 49 flat reed stakes 21½″ in length and 28 stakes 25½″ long. Set them up for the base so that it will measure 9″ x 12½″. Weave 3 rows of diagonal weaving (see p. 53) with natural colored winding reed. Using the brown winding reed weave a herringbone (see p. 63). Work one row of natural color, a black herringbone, a natural row, and another brown herringbone. At the top work 3 rows of natural color reed in diagonal weave and finish off with Border 4, clipping off any excess length.

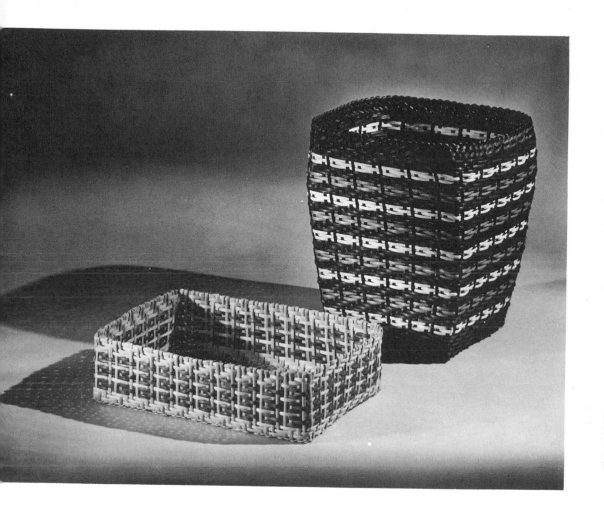

This wastepaper basket in its tri-color effect is quite striking. Reminiscent of Moorish art, it would fit into both the traditional and modern home. Not difficult to execute; simply follow the directions and maintain the gentle slope of the shaping. See directions on page 53.

Materials: About 300 feet of wide black winding reed, 53 feet of white, and 46 feet of tan winding reed. In addition you will need 6½ feet of black, No. 1 round reed.

Striped Wastepaper Basket

Height—12″

Cut 46 black stakes 41″ long and set-up the base 7½″ square. Be sure to keep the stake ends of equal length on all four sides. Complete a row of pairing around the edge of the base for rigidity, and turn the stakes upward. Work 7 rows with the black in diagonal weave (beginning at a corner). Place a piece of heavy, light-colored round reed in each corner to help strengthen them while you are weaving and to help you maintain an equal distance between these corners as the weaving progresses. This method will make it easier to form the basket in its proper shape.

After completing 7 rows of black, weave a white herringbone (see drawing); 3 rows of black diagonal weave; and 1 tan herringbone. Continue working in this manner until a total of 5 white and 4 tan bands, divided by the black, have been completed.

Keep checking while weaving to see that the pattern is correctly positioned—with the bands above each other in proper sequence. Finish the top with 4 rows of diagonal weaving in black and use Border 3, worked tightly to direct it inward.

Keep the form constant by maintaining an equal distance between the strong, inserted corner posts—beginning with 7½″ at the base; at 4″ up from the bottom the width should be 9″, and after 8″ are worked, there should be a 10″ width between the posts.

The last white row, and particularly the very last black row, should be held tightly, so the distance is reduced to 9½″ between the 4 corner posts.

After singeing, lacquer the basket two or three times so that it is satisfactorily stiffened.

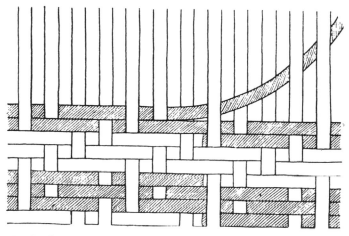

Herringbone.

HERRINGBONE—This decorative band is woven in 3 rows. The first 2 are a continuation of the preceding diagonal weaving (over 2, under 2), but at the start of the 3rd row, weave over one, under one and then continue over 2 and under 2. In this way the first and third rows are evenly aligned. It is best to begin this band at a corner or some other place which is not too noticeable, at the changeover from diagonal to herringbone cannot be completely hidden. See joining of winding reed, page 16.

Carry Baskets

For Instant Coffee

Height—to fit the can, plus handle

Widely in use today are cans or jars of powdered instant coffee which we use constantly for a quick "pick-me-up" between meals. However these containers do not look particularly well on the table, and therefore these little baskets with sturdy handles woven in "coffee colors" should certainly help their appearance. They should be measured and woven to fit the coffee container comfortably, in height and diameter, for easy removal when emptied.

Materials: The small size Carry Basket will take about 43 feet of brown round reed No. 1, 9 feet of black, and 16½ feet of narrow white winding reed plus 27½" brown round reed No. 5 for the handle.

The larger Carry Basket will use: 66 feet of brown round reed No. 1, 26 feet of black, and 36 feet of narrow white winding reed. For the handle, cut 39" of brown round reed No. 5.

Directions are given to fit the smaller containers, but the totals and other special instructions are included in parenthesis for the larger size. Both are woven by following the same directions, however.

Cut 16 stakes 15¾" long in brown No. 1 round reed and set them up, 2 and 2 in Base 1, diameter 3". (Cut 20 stakes, 19¾" long of No. 1 brown round reed. Arrange base B 1, but insert an extra pair in each direction, and use diameter of 4".) Weave with 2 brown, round reed weavers until the base fits the bottom of the can or jar. Check to see that it is really round. Then divide the stakes one by one with a row of pairing (see p. 17), and weave straight up checking the size to make sure it continues to fit the container. The best way to check is to place the jar momentarily right into the Carry Basket as you weave. Weave 4 double rows after turning the stakes to start the sides.

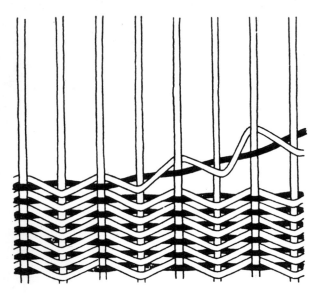

Pattern weaving with two winding reeds of different colors. Note that the dark reed lies flat in the weave, while the white reed forms a loose zigzag over the stakes to create the angular pattern.

Change to black and white winding reed. Beginning with the white, weave alternately with both white and black—see drawing.

Allowing the white to form a zigzag over the stakes and keeping the black weaver straight, will result in the amusing, serrated pattern shown in the photograph and on the drawing, but a constant check must be kept on the size.

When you have done 9 white and 8 black rows, again weave 2 or 3 double rows with 2 brown round reed weavers (18 white, and 17 black rows, then approx. 4 double rows.) It is difficult to say precisely how many double rows there should be at the top, but you might plan on having the last brown row about 1/8″ below the level of the top of the container. Finish with border B 2, woven horizontally.

For the handle use No. 5 brown round reed and cut one piece 15½" long and one 12" long (24" and 15½"). Insert the long round reed down through the woven sides (using a knitting needle or similar tool) to the lowest part of the brown band. Insert the short piece next to this but only as far as it reaches holding it even with the first reed. Wind the handle with white winding reed, weaving-in a black reed over one, and under one, etc. (See p. 32). Form the handle so it is slightly squared at the top as it is in the illustration. Glue the handle into place.

This round reed basket is perennially in style and can be decorated both inside and out with a fabric lining, flowers, sequins, ribbons, etc. threaded through or sewn to the weave. It has a two-tone pattern woven here in black (rear weaver), and white (forward weaver). Its lid is held in place by means of an extra border edge, and after it is woven, add decorations to suit your fancy.

The very dominant striped weave will be apparent, however, even if it is woven in natural reed with white, and you may prefer to leave it unadorned.

Handbag with Lid

(Wood base)

Height without handle—9½"

With handle—18½"

(See photograph—p. 69)

Materials: An oval wooden base, approx. $5\frac{1}{8}''$ x $10\frac{5}{8}''$ with 42 holes. Note: this pattern uses an even number of holes. If your wooden base has an uneven total, you must drill another hole otherwise this two-tone color pattern cannot be worked.

Brown: 73 feet of round reed No. 3; 116 feet of round reed No. 2; and 18 feet of wide winding reed. Also: 155 feet of black and 165 feet of white round reed No. 2.

Handle: 3 pieces of round reed No. 7, $39\frac{1}{2}''$ long.

Cut 42 stakes $17\frac{3}{4}''$ in brown No. 3 round reed, insert them in the holes, and weave the base border (see p. 18). Weave 4 double rows with brown. Two weavers must be used with the even number of stakes. Change, now weaving with one brown and one white weaver and alternate them to make the striped pattern where the white is forward with the brown in back. Weave loosely enough so that the basket will curve outward slightly. When you have reached 7″ above the base the circumference should be about 34″. Weave 44 black and 44 white rows in all. When the basket measures $7\frac{1}{8}''$ high, begin to weave it more tightly so that it turns inward evenly.

Finish with 6 brown double rows and Border B 2, which is woven perpendicularly, inside the basket.

HANDLES: With the aid of a rigid tool insert the handle ends at a point where the top of the handbag turns inward at the sides of the basket and about 4¾" down into the weave.

The arch of the handle itself should then be about 30" long. Wrap the handle with brown winding reed alternating over and under the 3 inserted round reed pieces, 2 white and 1 black (see drawing).

Weaving the handle.

LID: Cut 6 stakes 27½" long and 10 stakes 23½" long of brown, No. 2 round reed. Set-up the base to a length of 3¾" as shown in drawing. With the two brown, round reed weavers work around until the lid measures 1½" x 5¾".

Change to one black and one white, round reed weaver, and continue to weave over the stakes one at a time until the size is that of the inner, top circumference of the basket. Change to the brown reed and weave 4 double rows, then turning them back, insert each of the stakes down alongside its neighboring stake through the brown edge only, and out at the back edge of the lid where they are then bent sharply upward. A border should now be woven which is at right angles to the back surface of the lid (Border B 2 without the beginning stage, p. 25). Clip the stake ends off on the inner side.

Sew the lid along one side with raffia, or preferably, bast. It is a good idea to stain any part of the raw wood base that shows—to match the brown color of the reed. Line the handbag with some attractive fabric making a patch pocket to hold small items. Bows, flowers, small needlepoint embroideries or any decoration can be added to the finished handbag.

70

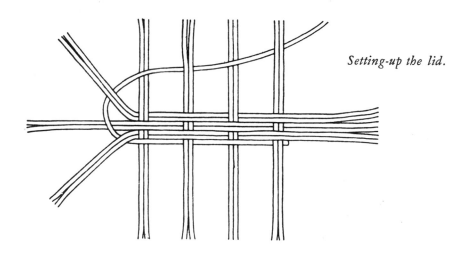

Setting-up the lid.

*Base for shopping bas-
kets on pages 72-73.*

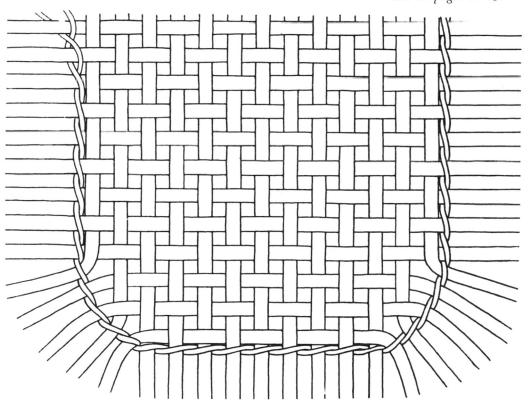

The small basket—7"; with the handle—14" high

The large basket—9½"; with the handle—17" high

Double-Handled
Shopping Baskets

The colors you select for making these handy, striped, large or small shopping baskets is a matter of personal preference. If you do not have colored winding reed, you can use a combination of white and natural, but the pattern will not be as apparent.

Materials: *Small Basket*—182 feet of black and 53 feet of narrow, white winding reed; 2 pieces of No. 6 black round reed 30" long, and 2 pieces 23" long.

Large Basket—231 feet of natural colored winding reed, 36 feet of black and 30 feet of wide, red winding reed, 2 pieces of No. 7 round reed 37½" long and 2 pieces 26½" long.

The two baskets are, for all practical purposes, woven according to the same directions. Directions are given here for the large basket, and include measurements for the smaller size in parenthesis.

Cut 13 stakes 39½" long and 27 stakes 33½" long of the wide, natural colored winding reed. (13 stakes cut 29½", and 27 cut 25½" of narrow, black winding reed.)

Set-up the base with 13 stakes and weave in the 27 stakes in the opposite direction—see drawing on page 71. The rounded corners should not be too difficult to achieve, but if they do not shape up properly, simply make a square corner as was done in the other baskets. Follow the directions for the base on page 53.

After a row of pairing, weave 4 rows in diagonal weaving using the color employed for the base. Weave rows of herringbone (see p. 63) alternately in black and red with 3 rows of diagonal weaving using the base color in-between until you have completed 4 black and 3 red stripes (alternate 3 rows black diagonal weaving and herringbone in white—in all, 8 stripes).

Inserting the handles.

Try to reproduce the plump shape of this basket. It should be woven to slant outward a little at first, particularly sloping at the ends, and then again slanting inward a little at the top. It will be more successful if you keep the stakes evenly and well-dampened. Finish the top with Border 3, tightening it a little to force it inward. Turn the stake ends back down into the inside of the basket.

HANDLE: Insert the ends of one of the long round reed pieces down into each "corner" of the flat sides of the basket, with about 23 stakes between the two inserted ends. It should reach down to a point below the topmost herringbone row. (See drawing.) Penetrating through the woven work on the inner side of the basket, it should be done as inconspicuously as possible. Holding the shorter piece next to the inner curve of the handle, insert it several inches down into the weaving. The curve of the handle should be approx. 24⅜" (21"). Position the other two handle pieces in the same way on the other side of the basket. Wind the handle with winding reed to match the color of the reed used at the beginning in the base of the basket then insert and glue the handle firmly to the inner side of the basket, as described above, clipping off uneven reed ends.

It is easy to get caught on the clipped-off ends of the basket edge, so it is a good idea to provide a lining in this basket, to protect both the contents and the basket as well; in fact a plastic material is excellent in this case.

This design was inspired by a primitive Indian basket. It is commodious and lined with sturdy material with small pockets around the circumference, it is an attractive and practical sewing basket.

Material: About 116 feet of both white and black, wide winding reed, plus 6½ feet of white round reed No. 1.

Cut 17 black and 17 white winding reed stakes 24″ long and set-up base with 9 black and 8 white in one direction, and 9 white and 8 black in the other direction (p. 53). Always alternate the colors. The distance between the stakes should be a little larger than the width of the winding reed. When set-up, the base should measure 7½″ on each side. Firm the base with a row of pairing and turn the stakes upward (rounded side out).

The zebra pattern is obtained by weaving with a white and a black winding reed, with the white woven over the white stake and the black over the black stake. It is woven this way all the way up. Be sure to keep the distance between the corners constant all the way to the top. When 16 white and 15 black rows have been completed, finish with Border 4 and insert the ends neatly into the basket.

For the lid, cut 17 white and 17 black stakes 14″ long. Weave the lid in exactly the same manner as the base of the basket, however, make this slightly larger than the base so that it will fit snugly over the top. After a row of pairing, weave with alternating black and white as was done with the basket. Do 4 white and 3 black rows for the overlap, keeping the size uniform to fit the basket.

Finish this again with Border 4; the ends worked into the lid.

Singe the basket and lacquer it, possibly twice, so it is smooth and rigid.

Zebra Pattern
Sewing Box

Height—6½"; width—8"

Zebra pattern weaving.

Globe Lampshade

Height and width—approx. 12″

This is a very interesting shape for a lampshade which does not diminish the light source yet the light will shine through the network of the shade throwing beautiful patterns across the room.

Materials: About 1¾ oz. round reed No. 5; and 1¾ oz. No. 2 round reed, both in natural color.

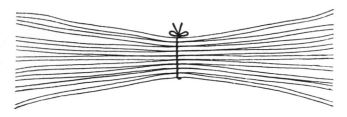

Tie the stakes together with a
strong thread and then weave it
in and out between the stakes.

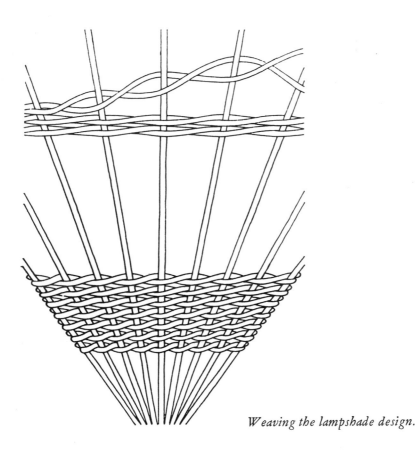

Weaving the lampshade design.

Cut 9 No. 5 round reed stakes 36″ long and soak them well. Bend them in the center carefully around a nail. Lay them out flat and bind them together with a strong doubled thread. Wind the thread around, and in and out, between each of the stakes in a type of pairing stroke designed to keep them from shifting out of place.

This binding together must not be removed until the shade has been completely woven. Spread the stakes out, keeping them at an even distance from each other and bind them with 2, No. 2 round reed weavers in pairing stroke all the way around, (checking to see that the form is kept round). Weave a total of 7 rows in pairing allowing it to fan out (see lower drawing and photograph). The distance between the stakes should now be about 1¼″. Insert the end of the weavers into the weaving.

To make the first band, do 3 pairing rows 1¾″ above the first woven area, and the distance between the stakes here should be slightly increased to 1½″. The ends of the weavers must rest on a stake. Now weave another 3 bands of pairing, again with 1¾″ vertical space between the bands. Allow enough room in the second and third bands so there is room for the two crossings between the stakes. The distance between the stakes, midway, should be 2″.

Weave the fourth band as the first, and finish the bottom with 4 rows of tighter pairing which will pull the form inward so that the bottom is approximately the same size as the top. Insert the stakes back, alongside their neighboring stakes (as in Border 1) and trim them. Now cut the tops of the stakes where they were originally bound together and insert these next to their neighboring stakes as was done with the bottom. Again use Border 1. This forms the top opening of the lampshade. Place two pieces of No. 5 round reed crosswise over the opening and insert the ends down into the woven section on each side, adjoining a stake. This will form the framework used for hanging the lampshade.

Glue all four bands of weaving in place and at the ends; hold them secure with plastic clothespins while the glue is drying. Put a drop of glue at every point where the weavers cross the stakes. A thorough lacquering will also help to make the lampshade rigid.

Construct the inner shade of parchment cut to size and glued into a cylindrical form using the same diameter as the top opening of the shade. Insert a lamp cord and switch socket so that the socket rests directely under the framework at the top of the shade, thus supporting the shade.

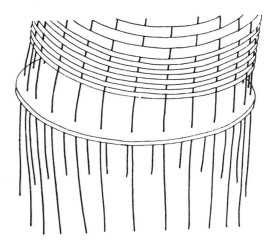

Use a wooden base with pre-bored holes to help in forming the lampshade when starting to weave.

This is definitely a shade for a dimly-lit, cozy spot. Its natural color gives a pleasantly warm-colored light, but because of the tight weave the light is only strong as it is directed downward. It is extremely attractive used over a dining table.

Materials: About 1 oz. of No. 3 round reed; 1 oz. of No. 2 round reed; plus 9 oz. of wide winding reed, all in natural color.

In making this shade, use a round wooden base as an aid in controlling the form; approx. $6\frac{3}{4}''$ in diameter, with 25 evenly-spaced holes around the circumference.

Cut 25 stakes of the No. 3 round reed, each $17\frac{3}{4}''$ long. Place these dry stakes into the holes so that $2\frac{1}{2}''$ protrude beyond and below the base. Do not weave a foot-piece, but begin with the top, constructing 14 rows of plain weaving with one No. 2 round reed weaver, and 40 rows with winding reed. When you have finished weaving half the required number of rows with the winding reed, you can remove the stakes from the temporary wooden base (see drawing) and the $2\frac{1}{2}''$ pieces can be moistened and then inserted into the round reed weaving (as in Border 1). Cut off any excess ends on the inside of the shade. When the 40 rows of winding reed have been completed, finish with 14 single rows of round reed and Border 2 A, which is also woven inward.

Cylindrical Lampshade

Height—$9\frac{1}{2}''$
(See illustration on page 79)

Office Letter Basket

Height—1½″; Base—9″ x 12″

The weaving pattern for the bottom of this basket is very unusual. This practical desk basket is intended to hold a good supply of standard-size typing paper, or the current day's correspondence to be dealt with.

Materials: About 3 oz. of narrow winding reed.

Cut 37 winding reed stakes 18″ long, and 55 stakes 12″ long. Weave the base with all the long stakes placed in one direction and the short ones in the other direction.

Keep the reed well-dampened at all times or it will slip out of place. To begin, weave 6 winding reed stakes together singly, one over another, as shown on the drawing numbered 1—6. Then weave 3 stakes close together (shown bracketed and numbered: 7, 8, 9, and 10) on all four sides of the first, singly-woven group. Continue the pattern in this manner to the edges. An individual pattern section will measure approximately 1½″. If you should find it difficult to hold the weaving together, you may use clothespins at the corners. Try to keep the other stakes, outside the weaving area, of the same length.

The entire base pattern consists of 6 broad stripes in one direction (with the smaller open weave between them) and 9 in the other. At the edge there are 2 single, winding-reed stakes in the pattern. When all the stakes have been woven in, the full size should then be close to 9″ x 12″, then weave a row of pairing with 2 thin, round reed weavers, and bend the stakes upward.

Weave the edge as in Border 3, but make it broader by going over and under a few more times, and cut off the middle stake of the groups of three which were previously worked closely together.

On the sides of the letter basket illustrated, there are 5 double rows with 2 winding reed weavers. Finish the top of the four sides with Border 4.

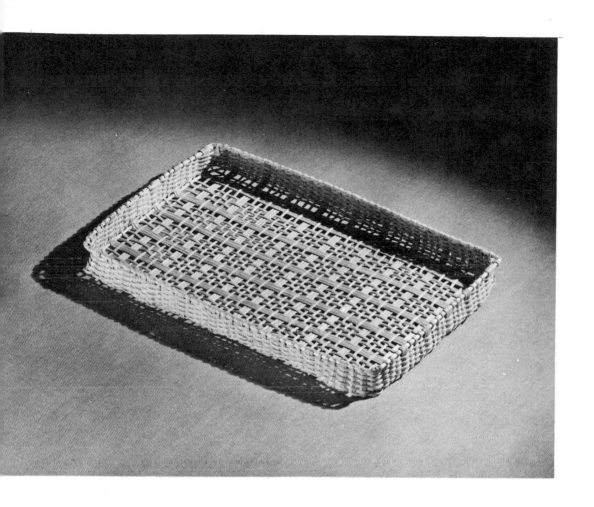

Chair Caning Pattern Procedure

Caning is done with winding reed, usually in either wide or narrow, natural color reed. It must be done carefully, but it is not as difficult as it looks, and actually it works up rapidly. The stakes must be quite damp, otherwise they slip out of position quite easily. The size of the hexagonal (6—sided) opening which results from this weaving pattern is determined by the width and thickness of the winding reed used, as you involuntarily (and quite properly) push the reeds close together as you weave. The caning pattern, as seen in the illustration on page 91, creates beautiful baskets and intriguing, decorative shadow effects.

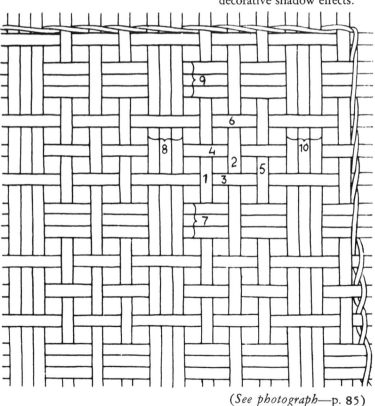

(See photograph—p. 85)

Clip the winding reed stakes and begin the weaving. As a rule, directions will ask for stakes of uniform length. The economies achieved by determining a more exact measurement of the length needed for each piece of this inexpensive craft material will not make up for the inconvenience and time lost in figuring it out precisely in advance.

1) Begin with a diagonal cross, something like an X (A-1 and 1; see pp. 88-89). Above and below in this X, weave-in two horizontal stakes (A-2 and 2). Then weave the required number of crosses on both sides continuing to weave-in the crossing stakes on each side of the horizontal stakes (A-4 and 4).

2) Then weave the next horizontal stake into the new cross A 4 on each side of the horizontal stakes A 2, above and below, so that you always, as we have done here, begin at the middle and longest row, and work yourself up and down from that position. You must constantly remember to weave-in the crossing stakes on each side of the last inserted horizontal stake, properly, close to each other. The opening will then be smaller at the top and bottom to form the interesting hexagonal shape. Always maintain a true parallel in the horizontal stakes (Fig. B).

3) When the required total of crosses in all directions have been woven, you can begin the sides in plain weaving, using a long winding reed weaver to weave-in the crosses all the way around (Fig. C), leave the outer stakes uncrossed as they are to be used for the edge. Tighten up the weaving slightly to get the edges perpendicular. You can, as suggested previously, use some clothespins to hold them, and remember to keep the stakes well-dampened. As there are an even number of stakes, you must weave with two weavers, which is advantageous because it is easier to hold them in place (D). For the finished edge use Border 3 or 4.

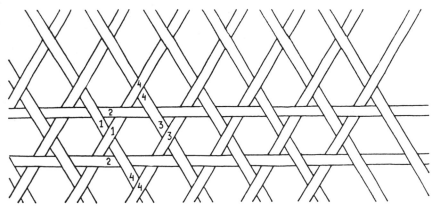

Fig. A: Setting-up the base. The numbers in the text (A 1, A 2, etc.) correspond to those in the drawings.

Fig. B: Weaving the base.

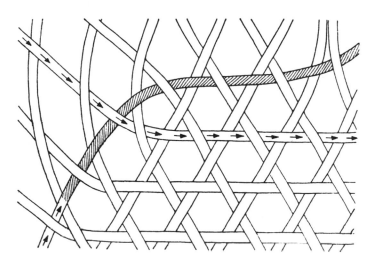

Fig. C: Beginning the sides of the
        basket. Weave with a long
        winding reed, shown here
        with hatching and arrows.

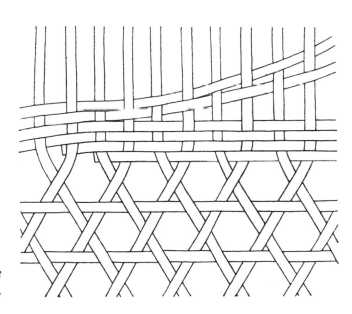

Fig. D:

Straight sides of the basket
are woven with two weavers.

The following directions apply for both baskets which are woven exactly alike. Where the small basket requirements differ from the large one, the smaller dimensions are given in parenthesis.

Materials: *Large basket*—approx. $1\frac{1}{2}$ oz. of wide, natural color winding reed and a little of the narrower winding reed for the border. *Small basket*—a smaller quantity of each of the same material, plus 2 pieces of No. 6 round reed, 21″ long.

Cut 36 winding reed stakes $18\frac{1}{2}$″ in length (24 stakes, $13\frac{3}{4}$″) and follow the directions given above for the caning pattern.

1) Weave 12 (8) crosses between the 2 horizontal winding reed stakes, and cross the perpendicular stakes on the outer side.

2) Weave in 5 (3) additional horizontal winding reed stakes above and 5 (3) below. There will now be 12 (8) rows of horizontal stakes facing in all directions.

3) To make the sides, weave with 2 winding reed weavers—preferably the narrow size—about 1″ to $1\frac{1}{4}$″ straight up and tighten the work so that the edge is perpendicular. Finish the top by positioning a long piece of winding reed over the extreme top edge on the inner side turning the stakes over this and down again into the weaving—similar to the method of Border 4.

(Make a handle of 2 pieces of 21″ round reed which is inserted into the straight woven sides and wrapped with winding reed. Glue it into place.)

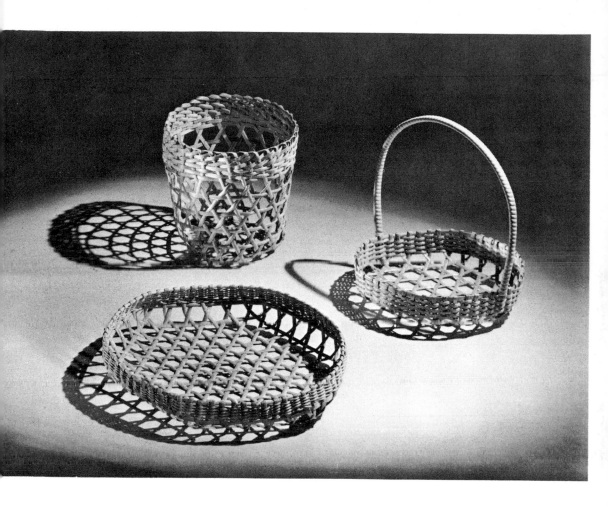

Flat Baskets in
Caning Weave

Large basket—10½″ diameter

Small basket—7½″ diameter

Oblong Caned Bread Basket

6¾" x 11⅜"
(See photograph, page 94)

Material: About 1¼ oz. narrow, natural color winding reed. Cut 10 stakes 18" long for the horizontal winding reed stakes and 34 for the perpendicular.

1) Weave 17 crosses for caning between 2 horizontal winding reed stakes.

2) Weave 4 rows of horizontal winding reed above and below these.

3) Weave 4 double rows with 2 winding reed weavers for the sides and finish the top as in the previous basket by adding a long winding reed to the top edge, controlling the oval shape in binding it in and inserting all ends when completed.

High Caned Basket

The tall basket is started in the same manner as the flat one (directions 1 and 2, p. 87). When caning of the base is finished, weave around with one long winding reed as shown by the arrows on Fig. C; page 89, and at the "corner" where your weaving started, letting the end of this winding reed weaver extend exactly as long as the base stakes. This end will then be used as another stake in completing the weaving, because here again, you will need an uneven number of stakes.

When you have made one round with the long weaver, continue by crossing the stakes between the different rows as you work upward in a flat spiral. Make sure that the sides are kept perpendicular or the pattern will become distorted as the basket is worked upward. In changing over to begin weaving the edge at the top, you must flatten out the last cross. Do not cross the last portion of the stakes at all when you start weaving the top border. It is woven with the same weaver that has been used in working the pattern upward. (See Fig. D; p. 89.) As you have an uneven number of stakes only one weaver is needed. The border is the same one employed for the flat basket. Trim stake ends off evenly before inserting back into border weave.

Follow directions given for the High Caned Basket, you will need about 1½ oz. of wide winding reed in a color to match your decor. It is helpful to lacquer this piece quite heavily to protect it when plant is watered.

Cut 18 stakes, 30" long.

1) Weave 6 crosses in caning between 2 horizontal stakes.

2) Weave in 2 more horizontal stakes above and below this row. There are now 6 rows of horizontal stakes in all directions.

Weave the sides upward with a long weaver; continue until there are 5 rows of crosses (see description).

Finish the top, weaving 2 double rows (Fig. D; p. 89) and use Border 3 or 4.

Flowerpot Holder

Height—6½" (See illustration p. 91)

Deep Fruit Basket

Top diameter—10¼"

Use approx. 1¾ oz. of natural colored, narrow winding reed. Cut 48 stakes, 22" long.

1) Weave 16 crosses in caning between 2 horizontal stakes.

2) Weave 7 more rows of horizontal stakes both above and below the first row. There are now 16 horizontal rows in each direction.

Continue with one long weaver, upward in a spiral (see description) until there are 3 or 4 rows of crosses forming the sides. Finish with 2 double woven rows (Fig. D; p. 89) and Border 3.

Weave this in the same manner as the letter basket on page 60. About 100 feet of white winding reed, 10 feet of red, and 10 feet of blue winding reed will be needed—all in the wide width.

Cut 36 stakes 18″ long for the basket using the wide white winding reed. Arrange the base with 18 stakes facing in each direction. After pairing a round, diagonally, weave 4 rows of white, a blue herringbone, 3 diagonal rows of white, a red herringbone, and again, 4 diagonal rows with white winding reed. Finish with Border 4.

This little basket can be used to hold hot breakfast rolls but it must be equipped with a rectangular, loose lining to retain heat. Following the inner basket dimensions, cut fabric doubled, with $\frac{3}{4}$″ seam allowance throughout. Sew four pre-seamed sides to the bottom. Blind stitch the top 3 side edges and insert a double fabric "lid" in the fourth side edge. This will form a heat retaining flap and the entire lining may be easily removed for laundering. A layer of thin foam rubber may be inserted to act as further insulation.

Square Basket

Height—3½″

(See illustration on p. 94)

The tea cozy is made in the same manner as the market basket on page 73, except for the different sizes, which are given here. It should be lined for insulation.

Materials: Approximately 233 feet of wide white winding reed; 35 feet of blue; and 25 feet of red winding reed.

Cut 11 white stakes 32″ long and 26 stakes 36″ long. Set-up the base (which becomes the top, as this "basket" is used upside-down over a teapot) so that it measures 8¾″ x 3½″. Make the usual row of pairing around the base, then bend the dampened

Tea Cozy

Height—10″ to 12″

Base Circumference—36″
(See illustration on p. 94)

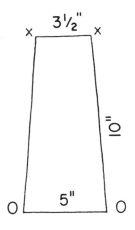

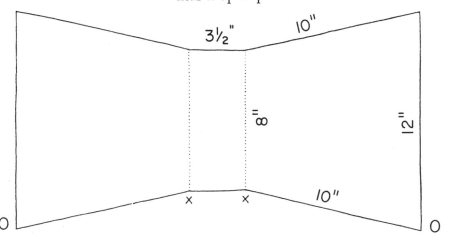

stakes sharply upward with their rounded side out and do 7 rows of diagonal weaving; 1 blue herringbone; 3 diagonal rows of white; 1 red herringbone and another 3 diagonal rows of white. Continue in this manner all the way until there are 4 blue and 3 red bands in all. End with 8 rows of diagonal white weaving. Finish with Border 4. Weave outward evenly, so that the circumference at the base is about 24½″ and at the widest opening it is 36″.

Form the small lifting handle of 2 pieces of white winding reed 7½″ long placed with their flat sides together and glued. When dry, insert it well through the white weave at the center of each side of the flat top as seen in the illustration. Glue it into place.

Assembly of lining: Cut 2 layers of the large pieces and 4 of the small pieces following the diagram. Sew them right sides together, matching x marks leaving 3″ open to turn fabric right-side out. Close last 3″ with blind stitch. Cotton batting stuffing can be inserted for insulation but a better choice would be thin plastic foam as it will launder as well as the fabric.

Stitch through the layers of both lining and stuffing in several points at random, 2″ to 4″ apart, so that the lining and stuffing will stay in position. Fasten the lining to the upper section with a few stitches to hold it up in position.

Pattern for
tea-cozy lining.